# JUST WHISTLE

## Also by C. D. Wright

*Alla Breve Loving* [1976]

*Room Rented by a Single Woman* [1978]

*Terrorism* [1979]

*Translations of the Gospel Back into Tongues* [1982]

*Further Adventures with You* [1986]

*String Light* [1991]

# JUST WHISTLE

*a valentine*

BY C. D. WRIGHT

*with photographs*

BY DEBORAH LUSTER

KELSEY ST. PRESS
BERKELEY

Part of this poem appeared in *Conjunctions: 17,* the tenth anniversary issue edited by Bradford Morrow, to whom grateful acknowledgment is here made.

Library of Congress Cataloging-in-Publication Data
Wright, C. D.
Just whistle: a valentine/by C. D. Wright; with photographs by Deborah Luster.
p. cm.
ISBN 0-932716-32-6: $14.00
I. Title.
PS3573.R497J87 1993
811`.54–dc20
93-11608
CIP

Book design: Mark Fox/BlackDog

Also by C.D. Wright

*Alla Breve Loving* [1976]
*Room Rented by a Single Woman* [1978]
*Terrorism* [1979]
*Translations of the Gospel Back into Tongues* [1982]
*Further Adventures with You* [1986]
*String Light* [1991]

The body, alive, not dead but dormant, like a cave that has stopped growing, stirred up, awakened, waked, woke itself altogether up, arose to a closed set of words, *I wish you wouldn't wear your panties to bed,* the body, on its flat feet, breaking into sweat, breaking into rivers, unbent at five and one half feet, having slept, as if in a boat, where the hair on its legs continued to curl long and gold, where its papers were stored, more or less dry, in a can, where whatever grew tired or useless fell off, fell away, having been not dead, but dormant, living, slept as if in a boat, oarless, unmoored, sand pouring out of a canvas bag,

Sand seeping from cavities no longer moist, not removing the panties, but making every effort to conform to the hull among scales, and leaves from overhanging willows, weepers, older than them even, wept, wounded into dormancy, unable to plug the wound, water deeper than night, the lewd, newly enlivened wound, night deeper than water, wound older than the body's marrow, older than its rocks, dogs glomming along the unstable rocks of its words, stirred up by days, sunblare, dreaded as the vulture dreads its own shadow; then, a slightly taller body waving from the shoreline with an armadillo on its shoulder, waving wildly as if for the pantied body to pull to rocky shore and share the armadillo, as if they had not crowed the night before

THE PANTIED ONE SAID NOTHING, not even its own newly enlivened name, its own naked name, the memory fulgurant, sheet lightning of other bodies, of the one that did not have a book in its house, the one that kept running to the pot, the one that admitted it loved the boat, the body stayed because it loved the boat, the impartial body, the inseminator, the second inseminator, the one over which the body had cut itself, just whistle cuts, the one that did not end after the aspirin incident but only much later during the war, our war on them, not the grunt the dodger, the one that ended in a hospital among neotenous bodies caparisoned in black, the first inseminator, the quick wit, that thespian, that did not attend the termination, the drop-out, the redneck, the uncut one, the juicy one a subway musician, the second inseminator, that did not attend the termination, the liar, the other liar, liar of liars, pants on fire, the gentle one, the only gentle one, the rough kisser, the one with an indefatigable hand, the all night rover, that readily laughing one, their combined tongues and clavicles, the two drunks, the original liar, so that even after the liar died, slew itself, eleven years after the liar died and had not a second's thought about its own rotted body

Much less the body in panties, the thinnest issue of piss seeping through, staining the sad panties a touch more, despite the cavernous question, so what was the big g-d deal anyway, why not repudiate the worst and resume, there must be a cure, some sweet acidophilus, poppy juice, a pill…, but that had to have been before the solecistic remark about the panties, which the body had not really noticed so used was the body to the cloth, the plight of their facticity, the elastic in the legs and the waist not being felt, the discoloration having blended them perfectly with the flesh, no line or hair, neotenous, and there being very little moisture, except for the thinnest issue of piss, it considered itself piquant; now this unmistakable run in the heretofore seamless nights, a disturbance as with a stick in the water, a seiche, this mention, this soft utterance in the dark where the one body could not be sure the other body was present but for the insistence of vowel points,

It was a definite rupture in the zone in which they interpenetrated with decreasing frequency almost without knowing it or as the one had been told of a flyer so virtuous the flyer could maintain zero gravity in our air, rolling a big jet without the passengers knowing they had been rolled, apocryphal or not, if a body coming through the halm were willing to help the body scaled and riddled with mistakes, to help the crumbling, hacky, runny body, the stiff, fitful body, the dumb, anachronistic body, the teratogenic, totally gnarled, hobbled body get to the other shore,

## In The Old Days

We didn't have this and we didn't have that
We rolled down the sloping shadows
Into the blue hollows like a bottle
Swallowing grass and stems
We fell into a nest of harmful bodies
We were pale and far as the sun
The harmful ones went sleeveless
Like trees without leaves
How we loved their smooth torsos
Like bluffs we leapt off
We loved them rough as boards
Hard as rocks we loved them
We had a voice soft and filmy as a mussel
We were like farm kittens
Each one different but the same
Our love was like the pulp
Of luscious fruit
We put up with a lot
Like living on Tchoupitoulas
That was the old days
Who could have penetrated the fog
In such bodies in those days

## A Brief And Blameless Outline Of The Ontogeny Of Crow

Tonight one said    Bluets the other said

Goosefoot one said    Hungry the other said

Hangnail it said    Spanish bayonet it said

Daylilies it said    Hotel it said

Matches it said    Sickle Senna it said

Feverfew the one said    Headache the other said

Panties it said    Panic Grass it said

Clotbur it said    Backdoor it would say

Tickets the one said    Purslane it would say

Morning glories said one    Money said the other

Whistle it said    Asshole it thought it said

THE ONE WATCHING THE OTHER ONE a long time before it got up, the one shoving a pillow under the plums of the other, the one not removing the panties even *in situ*; once this identical thing happened out west where so many beat families set down their beat gear and did their levelheaded best to get rid of one another, trampling the succulent ice plants; then *ex nihilo* the one who was asked not to wear the panties to bed was told to go check on the dogs

In the body's own words, it cannot live like a vegetable in the country, it no longer cares if it does die do, let them take a crowbar to its valves, let them open the howl of its os on the rocks, *why don't you go put your hands in some water,* the body is urged, but it chooses to celebrate its firing with a smoke

Its careless posture, its long trunk, its howling os, for so long it has been accused of bruxism, of failure to perform on the pot, of fulgurating, of hoariness, of bags; there are things which happen to it only at night, but the body dare not repeat them, the better to disguise its beastliness, while its ferns continue to brush their fronds off the porch, the cat cries and cries to be let out, then cries and cries to be let in, the body has been prepped, no need to shave everything, what doesn't take too long is over too fast, the body is possessed of childlike fears, predominantly flat fears, the armadillo does not respond to its calls, a phone rings and rings, the book opens, the letters take off black as flies, it fulgurates, love *avec* disgust, time divided by mercy, who is its shepherd, crow minus love, has it any wool, what on earth could be keeping it

Because conditions are ideal for crowing the singers flock to this spot. They rageth they seizeth they penetrateth and maketh us to lie down by the roaring waters. By day they take the longstem roses to our backdoor. They secure us to trellises. They whip us breathless. This includes the pool painter whose hands are perpetually blue. Aquatic. Transbluent. One hand signs the blued canvas of our body. Other hands. Cigaretted. Hired hands. Dripping paint on the plush carpet. They set a different set of teeth to each teat. Spit like grasshoppers. In the eden of their words, dogs glom. Warm winds stir them up. They let the flightless birds peck our feet. We hold mirrors. Bloody our lip under the rent in the backdoor. They crow us for the quick and the dead and on the third day they rise and crow us again. Very soon now we can return to our life of wonder and regret.

# Desk Cuts

I am incredibly sad

You bought a guitar
To punish your mother
You bought a kazoo
To punish your cat

    whacka
    whacka

I am a slave of the society

If love is blind
And god is love
And Ray Charles is blind
Is Ray Charles The One

    whacka
    whacka

BFS kicks major butt

O love like a meteor
Falls from such a height
At such a rate
Leaving such a hole

Now I am really stuck

    whacka
    whacka

Inseminate them

## Book titled *The Ballad of Sexual Dependency* Found in the Hydrangea In Front of Zorabedian's Stone

A photograph ripped out

If a fist of pennies is buried
alongside the bowl, the hydrangea
will grow blue

Zorabedian must be an Armenian name

Odds are a thousand-odd to one
the absent photo     was a crow shot

O the ballad of sexual dependency
is very old and intensely sad
we learned it before we learned

To bury a fist of pennies
alongside our bowl
could turn one's     abundant bushes blue

That Zorabedian was an Armenian is also true

Dusty apples in a dusty kitchen. Ferns brushing their fronds. Sound of water. Sloshing. Body atop an ice cream parlor chair. Finger tracing salt on the table. The body on its hinges. Midafternoon hysterics. What does the body want. For god's sake? What a lousy situation. A good whipping. A night or two in the pokey wouldn't hurt. To meet another body coming through the halm. Swinging its plums freely. Awhistling.

The body takes off its jeans in the barn. Washes its face in webs and rain. The hair on its legs curled gold. Checks to see, are its papers dry. More or less. Panties riding high. Checks the sprung trap. Stroking the little belly. Soft and still. The other body asleep in its fields. The armadillo on its sleeve. The indelible smell of the harmful ones. Not the one who worked for the highway department painting the center line. Yellow glo-paint coating its hands. The bold yellow signature on the gessoed canvas of the body. The musty undies below the waist. Ladder to the loft. Barn light. Bestirred. Benastied. Crow.

The one went so far as to send away for another body in the mail. The response was overwhelming. The one poured over the contents in the bathroom. Sound of water sloshing. Settling for the time being on an ascetic dish from France. The prevailing respondent wasn't French but frenched and smoke-free. The settlement was supernumerary as in the famous rib of lore. The initiator was inclined toward limerance, a delicious, venial condition [which is achieved without reflection or consent and so according to Thomist theology does not deprive the soul of sanctifying grace] nonetheless causing widespread perturbation in the system of the body left akitchen gnawing on its hinges.

GLARINGLY INSIGNIFICANT. Predominantly flat fears. Go put your hands in some water. Light a fart. They all rise up and leave their hairs on the pillowcase. They all enter breath's cul-de-sac in their own precious time. The body does not mourn its former bodies. The body leaves it ossuary for others to tend. Yet the body leans back on the trunk of an old friend, and says, because it is beautiful here, because it is so grotesque, because it is useless, vitiate it, slay it here. Now.

Followed by another closed set of words, *I just want you to last,* when already the unlasting has started, ruts have formed, petichiae, bags, dents, lacunae, sloughing, discharge, rot, the blaze between the cheek and the jaw, gouged out areas, new growths, horrible excrescency, discoloration, elongated lobes, the build-up of wax, crud, the degenerate mortar of lime, hair and dung, whilst the beckoning of the thousand-odd boats in the bay, the glisten and alternate glow of a fresh brain pan in a fresh apron, the identical age, not one cold flick nor hot lick older, its neotenous allure, doll-like, not a museum, no old familiar crow, predominantly young and manifest, with its thousand-odd reifications of its own solid grey matter, wielding authority, improvements in every direction, advances, actual sea lions at sunset, their seductive facticity, meanwhile the body on its pantied hinges in its kitchen, biting into its dusty apple, gnawing around the worms, wondering if it couldn't be useful yet going door to door

Advance of the distinct bodies behind the partition, the death of day, the rupture of motors, contamination of news, lightblare, sloshing sound, the time-honored tool ever alert under its suit, the long-maligned tube manufacturing trouble under its folds, the frisson of their proximity, the ineluctable concussion

The body is a suspect
in the offense of crow. It has the right
to remain naked. It does
not have to give a statement or answer any questions.
If it gives up its right
to remain naked, anything it touches
can and will be touched against it
on a floor of needles and moss. It is the forest's
hoary wife. It has the right

to the presence of a crow
and to talk with the crow
before and during its coring.
If it cannot afford a crow
and it wants one, one will be anointed for it
at no cost to it before any coring.
If it does talk to the big guns it can stop
at any time.

The big guns made no threats
or promises to it. The body understands
its rights. It is a suspect.

According to the author of *Points*
*for a Compass Rose* all of us are
defined by three transcendental
experiences: sexuality, aesthetics
and violence. Given the world
is not mean it is brutal,
Rosa's death comes to mind.
Who cut her teeth on cane. In the halm.
Her breasts hacked off.
She voided into her apron. They closed in.
Crowed. Slew her in the halm. She was flenced.
We, the transcendentally defined, climbed
back into our rental car.
Given we do not heal but harden,
our eyelids pushed down as if by a big darkness.

No. It worst. Destroys. None. Possibility. Pitched. Of. Friendship. Past. With. Pitch. Others. Of. It. Grief. Insures. Its. More. Isolation. Pangs. It. Will. Neglect. Its. Schooled. Body. At. Abandoned. Forepangs. No. Wilder. Longer. Wring. Is. Comforter. Anything. Where Few. Where. Crimes. Is. Entail. Your. Worse. Comforting. Punishment. Cries. Than. Heave. Generous. Herds-long. Fault. Huddle. Of. Woe. Putting. World-sorrow. Oneself. On. Entirely. Age-old. In. Anvil. Another's. Wince. Hands. And. Where. Sing. Where. Sing. Is its shepherd. And. What. Is. What is. The Thing. Keeping. It.

WHILST THE ONE BODY referred to its wound as IT another designated it THE THING. Both bodies did long battles with their wound and the body referring to its wound as IT slew itself on the eve of its own birthday whilst the one designating its agony THE THING gave birth to itself, took its children in hand and visited the sea. Very likely IT and THE THING are one and the same. Very like the felo-de-se had access to something the parthenogeneticist did not. Had the felo-de-se held out a little longer, the fog would have dutifully burned off, and it too could have visited the sea. In the old days, picnics, socials, public whippings, hangings and spelling bees were amusements in which the entire family could partake. But no one, in those days, able of body and soul, stood up in its saddle and let loose with a panegyric to its hole. At point blank range. At least not in mixed company.

Hole of holes: world in the world of the os, an ode, unspoken, hole in its infancy, uncuretted, sealed, not yet yielded, nulliparous mouth, girdle against growth, inland orifice, capital O, pore, aperture to the aleph, within which all, the over-stocked pond, entrance to vast funnel of silence, howling os, an idea of beautiful form, original opening, whistling well, first vortex, an idea of form, a beautiful idea, a just idea of form, unplugged, reamed, scored, plundered, insubduable opening, lightsource, it opens. This changes everything.

And nothing. The body slept under the bow two nights. Propped up with an oar. Cocked its gnarly head and listened to sheet metal music. Birds swooped down on it. The rock on its chest getting bigger. The wind told secondhand lies, more lies. It felt a breeze enter its vestibule. The flesh had begun to grow over the elastic in its panties like bark over fencing. Several of its fingers fell off, fell away. Oh well. It would not end up like the others. In a typing pool. Splitting gizzards. If necessary a prosthesis could be fashioned out of lime, hair and dung. It could still crow.

## On the eve of their mutually assured destruction:

The body would open its legs like a book
letting the soft pencils of light
fall on its pages, like doors
into a hothouse, belladonna blooming there;
it would open like a wine list, a mussel, wings

To be mounted without tearing;
it would part its legs in the forest
and let the fronds impress themselves in the resin
of its limbs, smoothe the rump
of the other body like a horse's. To wit:

The whole world would not be lost.

Let the record show the body
has made identical claims before
though never in the wake of its flencing.

CONTRACTIONS THROUGH THE NIGHT. Further and further apart. Then not. Contractions through the following night. Contractions. Closer and closer. Then constant. Two fingers. Scored. A long hall of bodies propped before televisions. The rupture of motors. Contamination of news. Lightblare. A bed. In which to bring forth. Impossible to lie flat. Walk. Walk the long halls. Counting televisions. Impossible to walk. The nub of the bone rubbed. Incessant rubbing of the nub. Up to the minute machinery. Advance of the machines. Relief of rubbing. Respite of ice. Through the night. Rock on its chest imbedded. Getting bigger. Tremendous fall of rock.

## At The Lying-In

Spell your last name for me please
    P-a-r-k-e-r
What do you do
    I am a shipper
How far did you go in school
    10th grade
What does your husband do
    he killed himself
Did you intend this pregnancy
    You know what people do
        in pairs
Do you have any other children
    4 boys
Were any of those pregnancies planned
    We were just kids
        I don't regret it
Have you been drinking during this pregnancy
    Only rum & coke
Do you smoke
    I am trying to cut back
Approximately how much do you smoke
    Less than two packs
What did your husband do
    he moved rock

The corpse was in the bed. On its back. The eyes were slipping back into the head. The lids were shutting down. Entrance to vast funnel of silence. It was dressed in a white shirt and white shorts. There was very little blood. A few bottles of beer. Chicken wings on the end table.

## On the morn of

The body would shut its eyes like blinds
letting the nearly even lines of light
steal away from its sheets,
straight gold hair astreaming there;
it would close like a glass door, an ear, arms

To be folded without crossing;
it would seal its lips on the forest
and let the teeth impress themselves in the skin
of its fruit, feast upon the marl
of the other body like a wilderness. To wit:

Its whistling world would be not harmed.

Let the record show the body
has never made such plaintive claims before
except in the wake, the wake of.

Here that sad body lies with its rubymeated vestibule
receiving the breeze.

The other body, priapic as a cigar, rubs the dark-staining juice
on the aureolae.

Lights conk off as they pass.

*One thing, the panties have to go...*

It knows its rights it has been a suspect many times before.

Darkness parts the multiple folds about the hole. The windows
come down in unison.

Nevertheless, it is very perturbing all this business
with the cigar and the aureolae.

*In the first place, the panties have to go ere it is too late.*

First, promise this isn't going to be any mustache job.

*Ere it is too late...*

If a body really wanted to help a body get to the other shore,
first it would have to take the panties, go back get the body
bring the panties back and get the cigar...

Staple it to the armadillo,

THEN DIG. Curl itself up at the approach of wheels,
        uncurling as they spin off in unison.

The leaves are dry enough for a nest;
        the ground gives.

The body will be walking in hours
        though the shell will be yet soft.

It might ring the armadillo
        and thank it. Thanks [for pointing out

This unmistakable run in the heretofore
        seamless nights, a disturbance

As with a stick in the water, a seiche,
        this mention, the accidental

        eden of its words].

Pain without walls: progressive pain: effacement of walls: four fingers: cored: a lot of hair: the pull the pain: the reaming: exhaustion: the rupture: contracting: ceaseless pulling: pressure of rock on chest: hair seen through the vestibule: tremendous fall of rock: absence of space: of breath: lights conk out as they pass: plummeting like a meteor: in unison: vast funnel of silence: dark parting the multiple folds about the hole: spinning into darkest surround: final vortex: plummeting into absence: from such a height: idea of beautiful form: intense monitoring of form: lights conk out as they pass: beautiful: darkness: spinning:

the needle: the needle is in: fear of needles: old childhood fear: old predominantly flat fear: it is a very old very fearful child: it is in distress: air absent: fear: fulgurating: fear *avec* pain: radiating distress: *avec* pressure: wheeling through a corridor of light: wheeled at tremendous speed: the windows come down in unison: needle entering the spine: wheeling into steel light: it freezes: freezing in the steel light: it freezes: teeth clicking: slit: emptied: released: glossy god brought to the head: golden: gorgeous: great gust of love: shown to the head: gone: gushing blood: an actual flood: absence of breath: of form: a beautiful idea: expelled: blood sloshing down the steel stilts: blood spilling onto tile: seeking the drain: at such a rate: more blood: blankets: hot blankets and blood: teeth clicking in the head: limbs rattling on the steel: stainless steel music:

the fat apathetic clock on the wall: what country does this mean: *why don't you check on the dogs:* what language does the clock talk: see if you can count the bodies in this surround: blankets: a stack of hot blankets: thanks: thanks so much: is there a lot of blood: and blankets: is love king: is it The One: help count: the clock has something to do with the country: the country of blind kings: there are any number of bodies in the bright surround: then less: slit: emptied: expelled: released: move out now: let's move: every body let's go: every: body: gone: leaving such a hole

A PARTITION SEPARATES IT FROM OTHER BODIES: a calm is coming: the promise of calm is calming: the body a yellow and blue canvas: swollen: distended: yellow and blue mixed gives green: the other body wipes the leavings from the swollen distended body: not a word on the armadillo: the gorgeous god is set upon an aureola: loveblinded: they are: in the country: it is: golden: of the blind: they are: kings

Over everything: up through the wreckage of the body, in its troughs, and along its swells, tangled among its broken veins, climbing on its swollen limbs: a blanket of fresh, vivid, lush, optimistic green; the verdancy rising even from the foundations of its ruins. Weeds already amid the bruises, and wild flowers bloomed among its bones. Everywhere were bluets and Spanish bayonets, goosefoot, morning glories and daylilies, purslane and clotbur and panic grass and feverfew. Especially in a circle at the center, sickle senna grew in extraordinary regeneration, not only standing among the blown remnants of the same plant but pushing up in new places, among distended folds and through rents in the flesh. It actually seemed as if a load of sickle senna had been dropped. On the eighth day...

Is it. is it.
it is. it is.
an object of worship.
graven.
an object of contempt.
craven.
asshole it thought it said.
whistle it said. just whistle.

# Voice of the Ridge

Something about a hazy afternoon—a long drive
    about cedars spearing the sky
Something about a boy at a crossing
    about a dog missing a paw
    about buying a freshly dressed hen
Something about the locus of the dead

Something about a strange town on a weekend
    about large white panties on a line
About a table in a family-owned cafe
    an old morsel on the tines
Something about the owner dragging one foot
Something about wine from a jelly glass

Something about a hazy afternoon—a long drive
    about no purse no stockings
Something about unfolding the map
    about a cemetery that isn't kept up
    about grasshoppers—their knack for surprise
Something about finding a full set of clothes in the weeds

Something about a hazy afternoon—a long drive
    about hills of goldenrod
Something about filling station attendants
    the one blue hole in the clouds
Something about birds of prey—the locus of the dead

Something about the long drive home—a slow sundowning
    about the din of insects
Something about straight gold hair on a pillow
Something about writing by the kingly light
    in the quick minutes left before lips
    suction a nipple from wrinkled linen

As if a fist of pennies had been buried alongside its bowl, *at least it didn't have to be funny for this one,* its bush bloomed blue, the one rooting, eyes shut, not Zorabedian, one was just out awhistling through the Armenian burial ground, the abundant bush, bent to pluck the book of photographs, this ballad is known by all, crow shot ripped out of the middle, it is very old and intensely sad, the panties excoriating in their own precious time, a healing beat begun, sheet metal music, revealing the sunlit shaft, the glans, crura, the other body's extreme *soif,* the thinnest issue of piss, arid as the hydrangea, the other body planting its pennies, a soul kiss, febrile, acoustic, an armadillo waddling off on its own, the other body inclined toward shade, fulgurating, alongside the bowl, asking could it have some of that water, the other roused, if only temporarily, waked from its amniotic dreaming, unbent at five and one half feet, flicked the switch on its vestibule, *did you check the dogs...* suspicious, fulgurant, but passing through its fluorescent words to the perineum, perpetrator of crow, fueled by previous experiences, where crow nearly slew it, deadening pedagogy of crow, not feed on thee, no, for if a body meet a body coming through the halm, the boat aground, for all of them so loved the boat, site of their facticity, occasion of the angel's wee victory over the beast

It was so likelife it was uncanny

it had its own ontogeny

the sequestration of the suspect nearly over

it arrived like a blot-from-the-blue

it stayed on, a macula on the forehead

etiolating their days of wonder and regret

the big guns arrived but it was too late

it had no alibi

thoughts of its dying cheered us up

a soft utterance in the dark

a night or two in the pokey

years in a leaky boat

were nothing compared to the beat of this wing

The pitch of the body unbent

risen on an elbow its abundant bushes

its hills of goldenrod and especially in a circle at the center

sickle senna in brilliant darkness a fresh apron

in extraordinary regeneration touched against

a nerve of tender concern for its papers

its incredible fingers flattening them

one at a time a healing beat begun at point blank range

around the insubduable opening the leaky wound

seven inches down and especially along the edges of its realm

the frisson of their proximity, the ineluctable concussion

## They Sleep

with tenderness, wracked

heaving

outspread

## They Sleep

heaving, outspread

with tenderness

wracked

## They Sleep

outspread, heaving

wracked

with tenderness

C.D. Wright was born and raised in the Ozark Mountains, the daughter of a judge and a court reporter. Her brother is a psychologist. She has published six collections of poetry, most recently *String Light* [University of Georgia Press, 1991], which won the 1992 Poetry Center Book Award. Among numerous literary honors, she has received the Bunting Institute Fellowship and the Whiting Writers' Award. With Forrest Gander she edits Lost Roads Publishers, a book press. Their son, Brecht, is six.

Deborah Luster directs the North Carolina coastal folk life project with Michael Luster. She has studied photography with Craig Stevens, Keith Carter, Pinky Bass, Larry Fink, and Linda Connor, among others. Her work has been included in a number of invitational and juried shows, including the "New Women Photographers' Show" in Carmel, California, and a two-person exhibit with Keith Carter at the Light Factory in Charlotte, North Carolina. She will collaborate again with C.D. Wright on the Lost Roads Project, a traveling exhibition focusing on writers of Arkansas, the native state of both Wright and Luster.

The images created for *Just Whistle* are photographs transformed by the bleach and etch process called mordancage. Mordancage etches the print by removing the emulsion in any area that has been exposed and developed to maximum black. The visual result is similar to solarization in that it causes a negative/positive reversal, but quite distinct in that it produces a relief print: the gelatin that remains retains the shine and the black that is removed exposes the paper's matte. I am interested in this penetration zone, this edge of line and relief. Along these edges the bodies are gnawed and wounded; parts of arms, legs, hair are eroded and fall away into the surrounding space. The bodies, due to chemical reaction and physical rubbing, lie in wracked relief. My thanks to Jean Pierre Sudre for refining the mordancage process, and to Craig Stevens for his patient instruction and encouragement.

—Deborah Luster